Gallery Books
Editor: Peter Fallon

THE SECRET FALL OF
CONSTANCE WILDE

Thomas Kilroy

THE
SECRET FALL
OF
CONSTANCE
WILDE

Gallery Books

The Secret Fall of Constance Wilde
is first published
simultaneously in paperback
and in a clothbound edition
on the day of its première
8 October 1997.

The Gallery Press
Loughcrew
Oldcastle
County Meath
Ireland

ISBN 1 85235 193 4 (*paperback*)
1 85235 194 2 (*clothbound*)

Characters

Speaking Parts
CONSTANCE WILDE
OSCAR WILDE, her husband
LORD ALFRED DOUGLAS, his lover

Mute Parts
An ANDROGYNE
Six ATTENDANT PUPPETEERS, white, faceless
   masks, bowler hats, Victorian jackets and pants,
   white gloves, clappers

The parts of DOUGLAS and the ANDROGYNE
may be played by the same actor (Male or Female)

The Secret Fall of Constance Wilde was first produced in the Abbey Theatre, Dublin, on Wednesday, 8 October 1997, with the following cast:

CONSTANCE WILDE	Jane Brennan
OSCAR WILDE	Robert O'Mahoney
LORD ALFRED DOUGLAS	Andrew Scott
MUTE PARTS	Muirne Bloomer
	Eric Lacey
	Kevin Murphy
	Ciara O'Callaghan
	Jonathan Shankey
	Jack Walsh

Director	Patrick Mason
Design	Joe Vanek
Lighting Design	Nick Chelton
Stage Director	Finola Eustace
Assistant Stage Directors	Brendan McLoughlin
	Stephen Dempsey
Sound	Dave O'Brien
Movement Director	David Bolger

for Patrick Mason

PART ONE

A dark stage. The attendant figures, mute, emerge out of the darkness: white, faceless masks, bowler hats, tight Victorian jackets, chequered pants, white gloves, a cross between Victorian toffs and street theatre performers, stage-hands and puppeteers, dressers, waiters and Figures of Fate.

Out of the darkness four of the attendant figures roll a great white disk, a performance space like a circus ring, into place down-stage under a brilliant spot. (NOTE: the disk effect throughout may be accomplished through the use of lighting.)

At the same time the voice of Constance from the darkness crying: 'No! No! No!'

Then two other attendant figures lead OSCAR *and* CONSTANCE *into the spot, onto the disk, rather like hospital attendants with frail patients. All six attendant figures then melt back into darkness leaving* OSCAR *and* CONSTANCE *on their own.*

OSCAR *and* CONSTANCE *perform on the disk, circling one another. They are both at the end of their lives, he in frock-coat and hat, she in a cape, both unsteady and worn, both leaning heavily on walking sticks. At first the exchange between them is rapid.*

CONSTANCE No! No! No!

OSCAR I must see them! They're my children, too, Constance.

CONSTANCE I've never denied that — that's *not* what this is about!

OSCAR *(Deliberate shift: nervous, uncertain)* Let's see — Cyril's birthday is June the fifth, isn't it? A twelve year old already! And Vyvie will be what? My God, is it eleven? In November?

CONSTANCE Stop it, Oscar! Stop it!

OSCAR What? What?

CONSTANCE Playacting!

OSCAR — not playacting!

CONSTANCE You never face the situation as it really is. Never!

Nothing exists for you unless it can be turned into a phrase. For once, would you say it as it actually is, Oscar!

OSCAR (*Low*) I must see them. Before I die. That's all. Why are you doing this to me? Why? Why?

CONSTANCE Protection —

OSCAR Protection! My two little boys are protected from me, is it? Because I'm a pervert? Is that it? A gaol-bird? Two years hard labour in the clink for gross indecency with male persons known and unknown.

CONSTANCE Don't, Oscar.

OSCAR Don't, Oscar! I can't touch my little boys because I'm a poof, a Marjorie, a Mary Ann. A prick lover. All you see is the invert. Barren. Yes! They cannot breed. So! Let them be without children. That's it, isn't it?

CONSTANCE Funny. A few years ago I wouldn't have known what you're talking about. And a few months ago I would have been sickened by such offensive language. How I've changed simply by living with you!

OSCAR (*Yell*) Say it as it really is, Oscar! That's what you want, isn't it? Say it as it really is, Oscar! Constance the realist!

CONSTANCE Don't bully, Oscar. It makes you seem tiresome. Besides you know it doesn't work with me. Actually, what I really want now is to face myself, to face, finally, what it was that made me end up like this. Here. With you. I want to face my own role in this whole sorry — spectacle.

OSCAR What on earth are you talking about?

CONSTANCE Evil.

OSCAR Evil? Evil! You know, Constance, you positively drip with goodness. You drench everyone around you with your virtue. Drip, drip, drip. Wet, wet, wet. Just like your sanctimonious relatives. Aunt Mary and Cousin Lizzie. Lizzie Busybody. Leaky, that's what you are, Constance. You leak, drowning in that wet, deadly morality of yours.

CONSTANCE (*Surprised*) Why, I'm not at all like that! You know perfectly well that I find that sort of thing — comic —

OSCAR (*Pause*) I am sorry. That was utterly inexcusable of

me. Sorry. I've had that word evil thrown in my face by every Tom, Dick and Harry and now coming from you of all people!

CONSTANCE You know you're the most self-obsessed, self-indulgent, self-self-self person that I have ever — I wasn't talking about you, for heavensakes! I was talking about myself!

OSCAR I don't understand —

CONSTANCE Evil! In me! Which I've never been able to confess.

OSCAR You're not evil, Constance —

CONSTANCE No, Oscar, not that, not anymore. Never again will I be invented as the good woman. Never! Constance who never screamed aloud at what was being done to her, the good woman who ran with her children, away from the horror, the filth; the good wife who kept him in money throughout even while he betrayed her. No. I want myself restored to me now. As I really am! Even if it is to be at the very end.

OSCAR But you always acted out of — goodness.

CONSTANCE Most times I acted out of rage! Rage! Deep, silent rage! Oh, it was so easy to appear meek, so easy. It was like dressing to go outdoors. One felt — safe. But it was always different when one was alone in the house. Do you know, sometimes I broke things. But you wouldn't have noticed, Oscar, would you?

OSCAR You mustn't punish yourself like this, Constance, mustn't!

CONSTANCE Why did you like having the good woman as your wife, Oscar? Have you ever asked yourself that? Have you? Did it make your wretched debauchery more easy? Hm? Did it somehow — protect you?

OSCAR We had — happiness —

CONSTANCE I think we were imprisoned by happiness.

OSCAR What on earth do you mean?

CONSTANCE Do you remember in the early days? How we wouldn't leave the house for days on end? Our House Beautiful! People would ask: Where on earth have you two been for the past few days? And we would smile at one another across the room. I thought no one is as tender, as loving, as exquisite, as mysterious as this man, and he is mine! He is my prisoner in this white palace. Then one day, I remember the moment exactly, I saw your face actually change —

OSCAR Please, Constance —

CONSTANCE Dripping with goodness, did you say? Wet, indeed! How you turned away from me with that stylish disgust of yours! I blamed myself, of course, lying there in the darkness. Women always do. Thinking in the night. What is wrong with me? Why is he unable to look me in the face in the act of love? Why does he make me turn my back on him, on all fours, like an animal when all I want to do is look into his eyes.

OSCAR It was not like that!

CONSTANCE And when I conceived with Cyril I will never, never forget that look of revulsion on your face, the disgust at what my body had become. When I tried to touch you you sprang away from me as if from something rancid.

OSCAR (*Cry*) Oh, God of Creation, what you have given us to live with! (*Shift*) What is — mysterious is that none of this makes any difference to my love for you. Or the children. (*Discovery*) There is so much truth in failure and destruction.

CONSTANCE At least you've sometimes expressed the truth to me, Oscar. Even when you surrounded me with lies.

OSCAR (*Heavy irony*) The problem with *my* marriage is that my wife understands me — (*Rush*) You went back on our agreement. You sat across from me in that filthy prison cage and you promised! Yes, Oscar, you said. Everything will be the same as before. You and I. Cyril and Vyvyan.

CONSTANCE I've learned that nothing is ever the same as before, nothing —

OSCAR And where did you learn that, may I ask?

CONSTANCE From your friend Alfred Douglas.

OSCAR (*Shocked pause*) Bosie! What's he got to do with this?

CONSTANCE Can you really ask that? After all that has happened?

OSCAR I have nothing more to do with him! Nothing!

CONSTANCE Oh, really?

OSCAR You don't believe me?

CONSTANCE No, I don't believe you because on this one subject you are capable of endless lying. And you wonder why I must protect the children! This is ridiculous!

OSCAR Protect. The children. (*Working it out*) From Bosie! Bosie? Did he do something?

CONSTANCE I see! You believe he's corrupt, too, don't you?

OSCAR Bosie! What did he do? Did he do something to the children? Did something happen? Answer me, woman! By God, I will kill him! My own sons — What did he do?

CONSTANCE Nothing.

OSCAR But he tried to?

CONSTANCE I wouldn't allow it.

OSCAR It? You wouldn't allow 'it'? What is this 'it'? Maybe it's just something in your mind, Constance, hm? Thinking up something monstrous about someone else —

CONSTANCE Why did I marry you, Oscar? Why? Why?

OSCAR (*Long pause. Brokenly*) Because. We loved.

CONSTANCE People keep asking me: What was it like, Constance, really like, to be married to him? Of course, they're thinking of you-know-what. It's as if they are undressing me with their eyes. Why, I answer them in my best wifely voice, it was theatre, m'dears, theatre! Theatre all the way! You know what Oscar is like! Every day a different performance. With frequent costume changes, of course. They are also wondering although they never ask: *When did she know?* All those young men and boys about the place. All those late dinners in Kettners and the Café Royal. When you consorted with sodomites and — what's that curious term? Rent boys! You didn't become someone else. You were the same person I had married. What is more, you were the same person I had wanted to marry. What does that say, Oscar? About us? About me?

OSCAR Why *did* you marry me, Constance?

CONSTANCE I fear that I may be about to find out. (*She suddenly doubles up in pain*)

OSCAR Constance! Are you in pain?

CONSTANCE (*Breaking*) I fell —

OSCAR I know that, dear. You were alone —

CONSTANCE Alone. In the house. I fell. Or flew. Down flights. Our House Beautiful, oh, Oscar! Number 16 Tite Street in the Borough of Chelsea. The most desirable, the most sought after entrée in London!

OSCAR Are you in constant pain?

CONSTANCE There are times when I cannot walk.

OSCAR And will they operate again?

CONSTANCE They say there's little point. The injury — paralysis is progressive. What a word. Progressive. You used to use that word of me, Oscar. Remember? My wife is progressive! She campaigns for Peace, the dockers, Rational Dress and Lady Sandhurst. A modern woman, my wife. Remarkably broad-minded, I must say. Progressive. Paralysis. Do you really care about my pain?

OSCAR Of course I care. Terribly.

CONSTANCE I've decided something about you. I said this to someone the other day. He's absolutely deficient, I said, in certain areas of feeling. And absurdly intense in others. A sort of imbalance that is extremely dangerous. If you have anything to do with him, that is. That's what I said.

OSCAR (*Pause*) Constance. What actually happened to you? On that staircase?

CONSTANCE Don't wish to speak about it —

OSCAR But something happened?

CONSTANCE — fall —

OSCAR But something else?

CONSTANCE — on the landing —

OSCAR What was it, Constance?

CONSTANCE (*Whisper. In tears*) Unspeakable. Evil. Crouching there on the landing. Squat. Evil.

OSCAR What did you see, Constance?

CONSTANCE I cannot tell you!

OSCAR Please —

CONSTANCE No! It cannot be told. It can only be — discovered.

Revealed.

OSCAR Please confide in me, Constance! Please! Don't you see? If you did it would — save me. Talk to me, Constance! Otherwise I'm finished. Back on the streets. Alone.

CONSTANCE But firstly, firstly it has to be — acted out. Then I will be able to face it. They're waiting for us, Oscar.

OSCAR (*Frantic*) No — no. Tell me, Constance. Please!

CONSTANCE They're waiting for us, Oscar. Back there. In the darkness.

OSCAR (*Surrender*) Yes.

CONSTANCE Waiting to put us through our paces. One more time. To perform. This time to face it as it really was!

OSCAR See how we've both ended up on sticks, Constance. How demeaning! Used to admire a decent cane. In the old days. But never as a mere aid to walking.

CONSTANCE There has always been your story, Oscar, but this time there has to be mine as well! You and I. Our — marriage. Our — children.

OSCAR (*Sadly: towards walking stick*) When something becomes useful it ceases to be beautiful. Don't you think?

CONSTANCE (*Shift to anxiety*) What's the matter?

OSCAR (*Desperate rush*) As a family we rather frequented the continent, did we not? Look how we've ended up! You with the children under the Italian sun and I alone on the streets of Paris. (*Pulls himself into the debonair mode, with difficulty and without complete success*) Each country exports its scandals. When in doubt take the boat. Otherwise life would be extremely tedious for the rest of the world.

CONSTANCE (*Now deeply concerned for him*) What is it, Oscar? When you go on like this I know there is something —

OSCAR (*Disturbed*) Simply cannot go through all this again, from the beginning, Constance. Cannot. Cannot.

CONSTANCE It is the only way in which I can go back.

OSCAR — cannot — cannot —

CONSTANCE — for me, so that I may face myself.

OSCAR For you —

CONSTANCE For my secret journey, Oscar.
OSCAR For you, Constance. Finita la commédia!

> *Loud clapping from the darkness around them. Lights up and for the first time we see the full stage.*
>
> *The clapping we have heard has come from the six attendant figures who stand waiting, equipped with clappers. All about on stands are full-sized puppets waiting to be used: two child puppets for the Wilde children, nightgowns/sailor suits. Puppets of several Victorian gentlemen in frock-coats, top-hats; of a judge and barristers; of a gaoler and policemen.*
>
> *A set of stairs which may become an elaborate staircase with bannisters, a court-room dock, a railway carriage.*
>
> *The disk is rolled back upstage by attendants where it leans against the back wall, a gigantic moon or wafer.*
>
> *The attendants lead* OSCAR *and* CONSTANCE *to either side of the stage, downstage and, there, facing the audience, they communicate with one another across a distance, without looking at one another. As they speak, they are transformed by the attendants into their youthful selves. When the canes are taken from them they straighten up at once, alert. Wig and costume changes complete the transformation.*

OSCAR Must we go back so far?
CONSTANCE We must go back to the beginning. That beautiful November day in Dublin. Oh, Oscar, you warned me! But I wouldn't listen —
OSCAR You were in love.
CONSTANCE And you, Oscar?
OSCAR I was ecstatic.
CONSTANCE Not quite the same thing, is it?
OSCAR Love should always have ecstasy. Otherwise it is in danger of dwindling into friendship.
CONSTANCE There are times when what you say appears so very

— limited.

OSCAR Good God! My language limited!

CONSTANCE Would you have stayed with me if I were a man, Oscar? I sometimes ask myself that. Then I say to myself you're bonkers, Constance, just like him.

OSCAR You're impossible, Constance, absolutely impossible at times, but you're also the only one to understand me, well my — feminine.

CONSTANCE Feminine, indeed. How could you ever understand what it is to be a woman?

OSCAR (*Attempted lift, reaching for the joke*) Of course I understand what it is to be a woman. Have I not been kept for years by my wife? Three pounds a week with the constant threat of withdrawal of allowance. How more like a woman could one be?

CONSTANCE (*Despite herself, she laughs*) Oh, Oscar, really, you are impossible!

OSCAR (*Lost*) When it began I was living in a dream of perfection.

CONSTANCE Nothing is perfect in this life.

OSCAR (*Testily*) Of course, women always know the limits of everything. Men seldom do. Hence the divorce court.

CONSTANCE You mean women always pick up the pieces.

OSCAR (*Annoyance*) You must always say something basic, mustn't you, dear?

CONSTANCE You mean real, don't you?

> *The costume and other changes have now been made and* OSCAR *has been given a new, very elegant, silver-topped cane. They have turned to confront one another. The attendants draw back.*

OSCAR (*Fury*) Real? Real! Don't speak to me of real! I abhor realism. People who call a spade a spade should be compelled to use one.

CONSTANCE Oh, Oscar, just accept things as they are!

OSCAR Never! Stand off! I may end up a decrepit Prospero with a terminal infection of the inner ear but not now! Now I can still — play!

CONSTANCE *does, indeed, stand off and becomes the
'audience' of what follows.* OSCAR *waves his cane as a
wand, a signal to the attendants who leap to attention,
acolytes in his ceremony. Music.*

*As he speaks, a 'statue' of an Androgyne, reclining,
naked, rear view, on a classical plinth is flown in or
elevated in, a moment of white magic to Oscar's
wand.*

*The 'statue' rises, poses, naked, arm aloft in front of
the great white disk. The attendants produce a scarlet
sheet and behind this the figure is gradually dressed as
Lord Alfred Douglas: startling whites, suit, shirt,
cravat and gloves.*

OSCAR (*A great yell*) I must have it! I will have it! Neither
man nor woman but both. Dionysus, the man-
woman as Aeschylus called it, descended as a
golden boy in whites into a London drawing room.
The great wound in Nature, the wound of gender,
was healed. And Plato's divided egg united once
more in a single, perfect sphere. Hermaphroditus
born of a kiss in the clear spring of Salmacis, near
Helicarnassus —
*Nec duo sunt, sed forma duplex, nec femina dici
Nec puer ut possit, neutrumque et utrumque videtur.*
Woman, this is our secret history, the history of the
Androgyne. In every phase of civilization there has
been this dream of perfection. *Cette gracieuse chimère,
rêve de l'Antiqueté!* A dream, a dream, you see. It is
the dream of Leonardo's *Baptist*, of Shakespeare's
sonnets, of Balzac's *Séraphîta*! And why? Why? Why,
because it is the dream of Paradise restored, the
undivided Adam, whole and intact, where there is
no man, no woman, no duality, no contrary, no
grotesque fumbling towards the Other because the
Other resides within oneself. But our frightened time
cannot bear such a vision. It curls away in terror from
what it sees in the mirror.
And so our age puts on its bright red uniforms and
goes out to murder its own kind. It beats its children

simply to keep the male and female in place.

(*The old frivolity once more*) Was it worth it, Oscar? some buffoon called to me the other day from the other side of the street. Haven't you noticed? There is always a buffoon on the other side of the street. Was it worth it, Oscar? It was worth it, my friend. Worth all the cheap jokes. Worth the humiliation in manacles before the gaping crowd on the platform of Clapham Junction. Worth the stink of carbolic and Jeyes Fluid in that cell, worth all the shit, my body rotting! When one sups with the gods one must pay the full price of admission.

CONSTANCE (*Scream*) But what about the cost to others!

It is as if she is almost about to strike him. Then they are separated by the attendants who conduct them, separately, downstage. During the following exchange DOUGLAS poses, an 'audience' to what is going on. Apart from DOUGLAS the rest of the stage, and the attendants, will remain in shadow. The full front of the stage becomes a brightly lit, autumnal path on Merrion Square, in Dublin.

OSCAR (*To* AUDIENCE) And so the young lovers met in Merrion Square where light is held in a golden net. And my mother sat in the window of the first floor, Speranza, a blue shade on Helicon, dreaming her mad dreams of Ireland. Or am I imagining it all?

CONSTANCE (*To* AUDIENCE) Everyone in Dublin was talking about him. Have you met the naughty Mr Wilde? Oh, you mustn't be caught in his company, dear. Certainly not alone. Certainly not without chaperone. I was suddenly, incredibly excited. Don't misunderstand me. It wasn't the scent of the forbidden. One had one's books for that. It was rather as if I were meeting someone out of my most disturbing dreams, half-realized, but now here it was, the thing itself. I immediately decided I was going to marry him.

Attendants take CONSTANCE *and run her into the lit*

space, whirling her about and she pirouettes, a young girl, a bird alighting. OSCAR *turns to her, comes and takes her by the arm.*

CONSTANCE Oh, how I love Dublin! I love this park, this square! I love Granmama Mary Atkinson for bringing me here so that I could meet you. I love the House Beautiful that you talk about. Will we live there, Oscar? For ever and ever?

OSCAR (*Putting a finger on her lips*) How brave can you be?

CONSTANCE What a strange question!

OSCAR I must have an answer to it.

CONSTANCE You're frightening me, Oscar!

OSCAR You must answer!

CONSTANCE But what could happen?

OSCAR That's just the point. I don't know.

CONSTANCE (*Pause*) Yes. My answer is Yes! No matter what happens. To me. To you.

OSCAR And now, my sweet, I will make my vow to you. You see, I believe that there is a fundamental essence within each person. Call it soul, if you will. It is what we take with us from the womb and to the grave. And it is very rare to know someone at that level. I know you in that way, Constance. I love you in that way. And that is why, no matter what happens, I will always love you. Any other loves I might ever have will be lesser because they will be contaminated by life. They will be of this world. Not you, Constance.

CONSTANCE Why, that's the most wonderful thing anyone has ever said to me.

OSCAR You mustn't forget it.

CONSTANCE I shan't forget it.

OSCAR Well, then, we may now talk of trivial things.

CONSTANCE Such as?

OSCAR Our blood relations for one. I was born of the union of a small, bearded goat and a walking historical monument. This accounts for the confusion of Dionysian and Apollonian elements in my make-up. Actually, I adore my mother. She is like a Celtic goddess in reduced circumstances. I despise my father.

CONSTANCE I don't wish to speak of my father.

OSCAR I constantly speak about my father. His behaviour is so dreadful that I feel I shall never succeed in emulating him.

CONSTANCE (*Blurted out*) Papa was arrested!

OSCAR Never mind, my dear. All the best families should include at least one convicted criminal.

CONSTANCE Don't be facetious, Oscar. Not about this!

OSCAR Sorry. What did he do?

CONSTANCE He tried — he tried — to corrupt the innocent.

OSCAR Which innocent?

CONSTANCE I don't wish to talk about it.

OSCAR You can confide in me, Constance. There is nothing that shocks me. Nothing.

CONSTANCE (*Surprise*) That's actually true, isn't it!

OSCAR Was it sexual?

CONSTANCE How on earth did you know?

OSCAR One always catches the unmistakable tone of silence surrounding sexuality in this great civilization of ours.

CONSTANCE Do you think I'm a prude?

OSCAR Certainly not!

CONSTANCE There are things that I cannot even tell myself. Then there are great blanks, cannot remember things; sort of — blotted out. Do you think you will always be able to tell me everything about yourself, Oscar?

OSCAR Absolutely!

CONSTANCE (*Deep breath*) Papa — Horace Watson Lloyd, barrister-at-law, practising at Number 11, King's Bench Walk was found guilty of — exposing himself in the gardens of the Temple before the perambulating nurse-maids. There! I thought I could never say that aloud.

OSCAR How extraordinary! We have been drawn to one another out of a mutual interest in patricide. (*She bursts into tears and he holds her*) Constance, dearest Constance! I understand!

CONSTANCE (*Shaking, through tears*) He gave me gifts —

OSCAR (*Puzzled but going with it*) Yes, of course, he gave you gifts. Mustn't punish yourself like this —

CONSTANCE Oh but I must! Mother actually dumped us, you see, after Papa died. Such selfishness! Do you know, I used to think that I'd be incapable of ever loving anyone, again. Until I met you.

OSCAR The past doesn't matter! Nor, indeed, does the future. Nothing matters but the immediate, thrilling present moment. We have to savour each moment to the full. That is what is meant by salvation.

CONSTANCE (*Drying her eyes, escape from her hurt*) Oscar! Tell me one of your stories!

OSCAR You mean — here? In the park?

CONSTANCE Why not? One of your once-upon-a-time stories.

OSCAR How odd! I really would prefer a stage, you know. Or at least a rostrum. Or even an interestingly decorated corner of a room.

CONSTANCE Oh, Oscar!

OSCAR I've always felt that the outdoors should be reserved for perspiration and the perpetration of scandalous relationships. Preferably with horses. (*Offhand*) Once upon a time.

CONSTANCE Ple-ase —

OSCAR Once upon a time. Yes. Once upon a time (*A shift in tone, gradually surrendering to the story*) there were three princesses. But their father, the old king, had sent them away into a cold, barbaric country. They had different mothers, you see, and the old king wanted to forget this fact so he tried to forget his daughters. But he couldn't forget. The place they had occupied in his heart became a blazing flame. His heart burned like a furnace.

And, far away, the youngest princess caught a terrible fever and died. They said her small body glowed even in death. And her two older sisters, who loved dancing, danced and danced.

But one night they danced too close to the open fire. When the dress of the first sister caught fire the second threw herself into her sister's fiery embrace and she, too, was engulfed. People came and threw the bodies into the snow outside but it was too late. Where they lay, a black hole burned into the snow. And back in his palace, the old king was finally free.

The fire in his heart had finally burned out, you see.
The end.

CONSTANCE Why, that's a wonderful, terrible, wonderful story.
How on earth did you make it up?

OSCAR I didn't make it up. It actually happened. It is the
story of my three sisters.

CONSTANCE I'm sorry. I didn't know you had three sisters.

OSCAR Not many people know. My youngest sister Isola did
die of a fever. And the other two — Emily and Mary
— died exactly as I have described it. In a fire. Dancing.
They were, both, if you will allow me, illegitimate.

CONSTANCE I see. So your father is the king?

OSCAR Yes. (*Pause*) King Billy Goat who sent his three
daughters away to die. Everything I write is auto-
biographical. With the facts changed, of course.

CONSTANCE I knew there was some story. People do talk.

OSCAR That is certainly true of Dublin.

CONSTANCE How awful for you, Oscar!

OSCAR (*Pause*) And how awful for you, Constance.

CONSTANCE No, I don't think we should talk like this. I won't
allow it. We're much too well off when you consider
how most people suffer —

OSCAR Will you be my sister?

CONSTANCE (*Fear*) Why, Oscar, we're going to marry. Aren't we?

OSCAR Will you be my sister, Constance?

CONSTANCE Do you mean friend?

OSCAR (*Fierce*) Sister! Sister!

CONSTANCE I don't understand!

OSCAR Yes, you do understand, Constance. You've under-
stood everything from the very beginning. That is
why you know what I mean. My sister.

CONSTANCE (*Slowly*) All you ever show to the world is this
brilliant surface.

OSCAR But you can see beneath it, Constance. Can't you?

CONSTANCE I don't know, really. (*Pause*) There are two ways of
knowing, aren't there? I mean there are facts and
stuff like that. But you can also know something in
your heart, even without facts. I may not know all the
facts about you but I know you in my heart. But do
you want me to see everything about you, Oscar? Do

25

you? I don't think you do, you know.

OSCAR doesn't answer. DOUGLAS applauds daintily and steps forward as well into the light.

OSCAR and CONSTANCE stand as if dazed. The attendants perform another quick, minimal costume/ wig change on them. They now become the married couple of the Trial years. The white disk is rolled forward into place again as an acting space. The staircase is also rolled forward, a full stairs with bannisters. The child puppets in nightgowns are brought forward by their puppeteers. CONSTANCE, back to audience, holding a puppet by each hand, slowly climbs the stairs, the puppeteers manipulating the puppets to either side: a mother seeing her children to bed.

OSCAR, away to one side, watches all this.

DOUGLAS (*To* AUDIENCE) Of course, one should always marry. Future of the race etcetera etcetera. Marriage is — how should one put it? Yes, a duty. Most certainly a form of protection, even a sort of — invisibility, if you follow me. But I did say to him: Darling, you married the wrong kind of woman. Know what I mean? I mean she knew too much. And then there were those two children. Made things frightfully complicated, the children. (*Short pause*) Adorable things —

CONSTANCE (*On the stairs with the puppets*) Time for beddy-byes, you two — upsy daisy — No, dearest, Papa isn't home. Do try not to pull on Mama's arm, Cyril. You mustn't say such things, Cyril. Papa loves you, loves you both very much indeed. (*Child's game*) Bobalink! Bobalink! Dreamtime! (*To self*) Dreamtime —

The puppeteers let the puppets fall and CONSTANCE stands a moment with them hanging to either side from her hands. Then the puppets are quickly removed and CONSTANCE stands alone on the stairs, looking up into darkness.

DOUGLAS (*To* AUDIENCE) Actually, I always liked Constance. From the word go. It was always so — well, bracing to talk to her. One never quite knew what she was going to say next. You'll see what I mean in a moment.

> *As he speaks,* CONSTANCE *has descended the staircase and comes downstage. She stands there, facing out into the audience.* OSCAR, *meanwhile, has begun to circle the disk in increasing agitation. The attendants place an ornate chaise longue on the disk. They conduct* DOUGLAS *onto the disk and seat him, delicately, upon the chaise longue, then stand in a line above the disk.*

Never know why the penny romances call this kind of affair a love triangle. Do you? Far more than three angles involved, wouldn't you agree?

OSCAR (*As if rushing through a house, yelling*) Bosie! Are you there, Bosie!

DOUGLAS (*To* AUDIENCE) And that's another thing! This frightful slander that's being passed about everywhere. I never interfered with those children. Never!

OSCAR (*Finally leaping onto the disk, arms out*) Bosie!

DOUGLAS Oh, it's you, is it!

> OSCAR *embraces him, kissing him passionately and* DOUGLAS *returns the kisses. The six attendant figures surround them completely, a heaving black coverlet covering the chaise longue.* CONSTANCE *pays no attention to this.*

CONSTANCE (*To* AUDIENCE) Sometimes he would return to our home in Tite Street to see the children but only when he believed I was out. I would open a door and find him there, the children on his knee, clasping him, this look on his face, a look at once of happiness and horror, those large white hands falling away from the children's bodies when he caught sight of me. 'Only a few moments more, dear,' he'd murmur, unable to look me in the eye —

The six attendants have risen and departed into shadow leaving a dishevelled OSCAR *and a less dishevelled* DOUGLAS *who rearrange themselves.* CONSTANCE *turns towards the disk and* OSCAR, *looking off, spots her.*

OSCAR   I really should become a gymnast! (*Looks off*) Oh, my God, she's coming here! Get rid of her, would you! I simply can't face her.

He moves off the disk and turns his back to what happens next. CONSTANCE *will eventually step onto the disk and* DOUGLAS *will turn to her as if she has just entered a room.*

DOUGLAS   Oscar! No! Dammit! Why, Constance! This *is* a surprise!

CONSTANCE   May I see my husband?

DOUGLAS   I should certainly think so. Wives see their husbands all the time, do they not?

CONSTANCE   Don't you dare mock me!

DOUGLAS   I am not Oscar's keeper, you know.

CONSTANCE   I want to see him. Now, if you please.

DOUGLAS   Well, then, you must find him, mustn't you?

CONSTANCE   I don't intend to search these rooms.

DOUGLAS   I am very relieved to hear it. One is very fearful of house-searches, nowadays.

CONSTANCE   Do you think I'm a fool?

DOUGLAS   Certainly not.

CONSTANCE   Merely a woman, would you say?

DOUGLAS   Do not burden me, please, with your self-doubt.

CONSTANCE   On the contrary, Lord Douglas, right now my doubts are about other people. You, for example.

DOUGLAS   Lord Douglas! My! No Alfred? No Bosie?

CONSTANCE   (*Actually curious*) Do you really have no idea of how much scandal is attached to your name?

DOUGLAS   I don't wish to hear it. I love to hear scandal about others but scandal about myself doesn't interest me. It doesn't have the charm of novelty.

CONSTANCE   Oh Oscar has taught you well. You even speak like him. Parrot-like.

DOUGLAS If I am his parrot, then you must be his hen.

CONSTANCE How offensive you are! I assure you I am not his *anything*. That's the difference between us. Apart from the fact that I am his wife. That is another difference. (DOUGLAS *laughs a high-pitched laugh, quickly cut off*) Why do you laugh?

DOUGLAS Nothing, Mrs Wilde. Mrs Wilde — Mrs Wilde. I have heard that soubriquet used of others, Mrs Wilde. (*Again the laugh, again cut short*)

CONSTANCE What others?

DOUGLAS Well, if you must know, a young man named Edward Shelley. For one.

CONSTANCE What exactly is that supposed to mean?

DOUGLAS Oh, God! Look here. I hate this ridiculous — fencing. It brings out the very worst in one. It makes me into a horror. I hate it. Besides, I actually like you. I admire you. We could be friends. I rather think of you as a sister. (*It is now* CONSTANCE's *turn to laugh*) What is it?

CONSTANCE Nothing. I just remembered something — sister — someone said something similar to me. A long time ago. Anyway, I don't believe you.

DOUGLAS Oh, but you must! It is the solution to everything.

CONSTANCE What is?

DOUGLAS One could keep things just as they are, you see. Oscar needs me. I am his inspiration. He needs you. With you he finds peace. He needs the children —

CONSTANCE I forbid you to speak of our children! Forbid you!

DOUGLAS Oh, dear! Look, it's wretched that you should suffer like this. There's absolutely no need of it.

CONSTANCE I don't need your sympathy, you contemptible person!

DOUGLAS I'll ignore that remark. What you need is a confidante. Yes! Exactly. Someone wise in the world who can talk it all through with you, explain things to you. I wish I could. But I cannot. It is all too impossibly Parisian! A wise counsellor, a go-between. Oscar will think of someone. An older woman, perhaps?

CONSTANCE What on earth are you talking about?

DOUGLAS Someone to help you —

CONSTANCE Help me? How?

DOUGLAS   To explain the situation, for heavensakes! Oscar! I!
           You! What is going on!

CONSTANCE But I am perfectly aware of what is going on. As you
           put it.

DOUGLAS   You are!

CONSTANCE Yes. You and Oscar are Urnings. That is the term
           used by the German expert on sexual behaviour,
           Karl Heinrich Ulrich. Are you a true Urning, Lord
           Douglas, or do you also consort with women? It
           is apparently rather difficult to tell. Oscar is a
           Uranodiominge, that is to say an Urning who can
           also live with a woman. On the other hand, the true
           Urning who forces himself to cohabit with a woman,
           simply to conceal his true nature, say, well he is
           called a Virilisirt. Oscar is not a Virilisirt, no, I'm
           pretty certain of that.

DOUGLAS   Where on earth did you get all this?

CONSTANCE From a book. I love to surprise people by revelations
           from my reading. My! But you do look a sight! Shall
           I fetch you some smelling salts?

DOUGLAS   A book! I really must sit down. I feel quite faint.

CONSTANCE What you have to understrand is that we women are
           trained from birth to conceal. Otherwise, you see,
           men would be unable to behave as they do. This is
           what is known as society. There. See? I can speak like
           Oscar, too.

DOUGLAS   I had no idea — I thought you had come here — I
           thought you were trying to sniff things out. I am
           utterly bewildered.

CONSTANCE Actually, I came here to talk about money.

DOUGLAS   Money! Money? Money!

CONSTANCE Let me list it for you. My allowance comes to just
           under £800 a year. Oscar, with your assistance,
           succeeded in going through £1,340 in three months
           — three months! At Goring. But I don't need to
           explain this to you. After all, you were there, were
           you not?

DOUGLAS   There are, well, certain — facilities, Constance Wilde,
           that I am accustomed to.

CONSTANCE Meantime, the quarterly rent is due on Tite Street and I must ask my Aunt Mary, once more, for a loan. Meantime, Oscar has taken yet another advance from Mr Alexander for yet another unwritten play. Meantime, we have put the two boys down for schools, Bedales for Cyril, Hindlesham for Vyvie, but where, pray, are the fees? Meantime, I turn my back and Oscar has whisked you off for yet another weekend in Dieppe.

DOUGLAS You speak of me as if I were a piece of luggage at a railway station.

CONSTANCE How apt.

DOUGLAS I will not have it, do you hear!

CONSTANCE And I will not have *my* money spent on *you*! You may say all of this to my husband, Lord Douglas, should he choose to make an entrance after my departure.

DOUGLAS Just a moment —

CONSTANCE Good-day —

She leaves but takes up a position beside the circle space with her back turned.

DOUGLAS (*Weakly*) But I like women — I really do!

OSCAR *steps on to the circle space as if from another room.*

OSCAR Has she gone?

DOUGLAS Do you love me?

OSCAR's answer is a kiss, followed by more kisses, his hands caressing DOUGLAS's body. DOUGLAS pushes him away.

Do you mind!

OSCAR What did she say to you?

DOUGLAS Do you know you married a remarkable woman? Constance Holland Lloyd. Quite, quite remarkable. Yes. Do you realize that she knows everything about us?

OSCAR Everyone knows everything about us, dear boy. Your

delightful father has seen to that, going about town with his lurid, filthy messages to everyone who will listen. I only wish we could live up to his obscene imagination.

DOUGLAS I don't wish to speak of my monstrous father. I want to talk about your wife.

OSCAR Not now, dear.

DOUGLAS But you constantly talk about her. Constance this, Constance that.·I find it extremely tiresome.

OSCAR I beg your pardon!

DOUGLAS Yes — letting her worm her way in — poking herself in — the way women always do with that whine of theirs. She brings you to heel. Here, doggy! and you trot along, on the leash! Why, Oscar? Why? Away from her you are utterly different. One thing in the country, another thing in town.

OSCAR No, I am not!

DOUGLAS Yes, you are! But you hate to face it. Double-faced, that's what you are. You hate them, women. You hate their smell. Mulierism. That's your word. Have you forgotten? I could never be a mulierist again, you said, tossing your locks. They are swallowing me up, you said, all those shes, sucking one in, slits, tweakes, digusting but no, no, Jesus Oscar must keep up pretence! That bitch!

> OSCAR *hits him. It is a shocking blow but even as the blow is struck* OSCAR *is ready to pull back again, to take* DOUGLAS *in his arms again.*

OSCAR Don't you dare speak of her like that! Ever!

DOUGLAS Forgive me, forgive me.

OSCAR You know nothing about her! Nothing!

DOUGLAS Why am I like this? Why — why?

OSCAR I tell you there are times that I return to that house and I am a piece of human wreckage. She says nothing, simply looks at me. She sits quietly in a window, reading perhaps, perhaps sketching, allowing me to play with the children on the carpet. All the mad, frantic pursuit of flesh dies down in me.

That room in my house has such perfect poise, such stillness, that I have a brief, momentary illusion of the state of grace. That is what she means to me! That is what my children mean to me!

DOUGLAS I am a monster. My blood is monstrous. Look at my father! Savagery. I am going to kill myself. It is the only way out.

OSCAR Do you know, it's rather as if one had stepped into a cool interior on canvas. Vermeer, perhaps.

DOUGLAS But for you I would have killed myself already. You know that. You are the only one who finds something — worthwhile in me. The only one! A reason to live. Then I do this. To her. Whom I like. I actually do like her! Like something pouring out of me, abscess, pus. I'm diseased. Cannot stop. I try, oh, I try. Only with you can I see some semblance of humanity when I look in the mirror.

> OSCAR *holds him in a deep embrace when he has ended. Then* DOUGLAS *breaks away, fully restored, as if nothing unusual has happened.*

What's that story about her father, then?

OSCAR Which story?

DOUGLAS Was he queer? Her father?

OSCAR Her father? Nonsense. Whoever said such a thing?

DOUGLAS There's gossip.

OSCAR Oh, it's gossip, is it?

DOUGLAS Don't blame me, dearie. I'm only repeating what is said behind curtains. By the way, she also asked me to tell you something.

OSCAR What?

DOUGLAS She said to say you were broke.

> OSCAR *laughs, a wild laugh of despair, and then stops short. Both he and* DOUGLAS *stand, drained, not looking at one another. The attendants applaud with their clappers. They remove the two men from the circle where they stand, heads averted.*
>
> *First, the mobile staircase is put in place on the cir-*

cular space. CONSTANCE *has been dressed in a peignoir, her hair hangs loose about her and she carries a bottle. She is conducted forward, drunk, staggering slightly as she wanders through her house.*

CONSTANCE (*Drinking*) One last sip, Constance, just one, teeny tiny one and then beddy-byes. There! What is it about an empty house? So — skeletal. (*Drinks in the words*) Shell. Holl-ow. (*Sudden briskness*) Send the children away to school, Constance. Much better for them, Constance, what with — you know? Much better for you, Constance, do something with yourself. (*Each beat*) Remarkable, truly remarkable, how advice, of people, always, seems to — flatter those people themselves. Smart girl, Constance! Plucky girl, Constance! But how do you manage it? Plu-ck! People close to him want to kill themselves. Douglas said that. Should know, he should.

The society hostess. As she speaks, chair, desk, dining-room table come flying by as if she were conducting a surreal auction, the attendants as auctioneer's help.

Yes, m'dears, that is Mr Wilde's chair over there, does all his great work on it, well, some of it. Used to, anyway. Used to belong to Mr Carlyle, chair that is, don't touch, please, thank you! And here is the white dining room with its famous white furniture specially made by Mr Godwin, old Godwino, a concerto in ivory, Mr Wilde's phrase. Mr Wilde's phrasing. A phrase for everything, Mr Wilde. (*Down*) Except failure. (*Up*) Oh, and do let me show you the ceiling of the drawing room. Just upstairs. (*The 'ceiling' appears above her head like a canopy, peacock feathers floating down*) Painted by Mr Whistler, no less. Notice in particular the two gold dragons with inlaid real peacock's feathers. Real! Real!

What a load of rubbish it all is! (*Very carefully places bottle at her feet*)

Funny thing, now, way people go on as if it were

the flesh when it wasn't the flesh at all. You see, if it were the flesh the flesh is satisfied and he was never, never, never satisfied. How do I know? Oh, I know! You see there was something in nature that he could never accept. Maybe that's why he could write such splendid comedy?

> *The attendants suddenly seize her and she screams. They drag her to the staircase and she struggles against them as they push her up the steps to the landing.*

No! Please! Don't! I can't go up there! I can't. Can't do it. Not on my own! Please! Where is Oscar? Where is Oscar?

> *She is now on the landing, crouched, facing the audience, drinking. The attendants retreat to the foot of the steps where they raise their white gloved hands to receive her.*

Nothing there. Empty house. Skeletal. No sound. Nothing. Safe. Constance safe. No-one-to-harm-her. See! Empty!
  Then I flew. Became untouchable, you see. I saw before me this — open — expanse — blue, so blue in all the whiteness of our house, House Beautiful. I saw blue and began to fly.

> *Music. She launches herself into the air and is held in the upraised hands of the attendants. They turn her body slowly in the air, a choreographed tumble, and she screams. Over and over until they bring her slowly down on the floor, still screaming, at the foot of the stairs. The attendants stand aside as she lies on her back in great pain. She turns with difficulty and begins to crawl off. The attendants follow her and only when she reaches the edge of the circle do they react. They first applaud with their clappers, then lift and drag her off.*

(*Crawling*) Help me. Someone. Please!

> *Music. The staircase is removed from the white circle by the attendants.*
>
> *Two elegant chairs are placed side by side on the white space.* OSCAR *and* CONSTANCE *are re-dressed by the attendants, minimal costume changes, perhaps a hat and cane to him, a shawl to her.*
>
> DOUGLAS, *meanwhile, has come forward to address the audience.*

DOUGLAS Actually I was the only one of the three who had the slightest control over my fate. With this one exception. The whole thing made me more vile than I actually am. As you've seen just now. Not a bad chap usually. Really. The other thing is that I needed more than he was prepared to give.

I cry out to him: Look at me! Look at me! I am human! A kind of glaze comes over his eyes. He presses money into my hands. I drink too much. I gamble like a madman. I lose. He presses more money into my hands. On and on! I am driven by this twin demon of idolatory and neglect. I have never been so attended on, never so lonely in my life. I exaggerate, of course, but you get my drift. And then I find that he is still slipping back to that house on Tite Street. To her. What on earth is he up to? He says it's to see the children. But every time he returns to me he is sunken in this black depression. What is she saying to him? Is she feeding him some dreadful woman lies? I must find out! Yes, I must!

> *He steps aside, off the white disk, standing with his back to what happens.*
>
> CONSTANCE *is led on, walking with a slight limp, and is seated in one of the chairs.* OSCAR *steps up onto the white disk behind her. It is as if he has just entered the room behind her and she looks up.*

OSCAR I didn't wake them. Fast asleep! So beautiful! I

simply stood in the doorway and peeped in. Cyril had all his navy arrayed by the bedside, flags aloft. While Vyvie was clutching old Snow Bear for dear life. Dear life! I am sorry about your accident, Constance. You must call on me at once when something like this happens.

CONSTANCE You know, I actually did cry out for you. On that stairs. Where were you, Oscar? In St James's Place? Brighton, maybe? Perhaps in the Hôtel des Deux Mondes? Or some other Parisian hide-out? Perhaps I could have sent a wire to Algiers? That's a possibility, now. (*Pause*) I want a divorce.

OSCAR Divorce! Is that why you invited me here?

CONSTANCE No, as a matter of fact. There's something else I need to tell you. But this sort of — popped out.

OSCAR Popped out! Popped out! Divorce! And that, I take it, is my cue to ask the inevitable, melodramatic question: Is there someone else?

CONSTANCE There may be.

OSCAR How suitably inconclusive. Who is it?

CONSTANCE Arthur.

OSCAR Do you mean Arthur Humphreys of Hatchard's bookshop? How thrilling. You and he have been arranging to publish my aphorisms while playing hanky-panky among the bookshelves.

CONSTANCE Why, Oscar, you're jealous!

OSCAR Certainly not! Indeed, I am pleased that someone has been in attendance on you. I am pleased for you. Besides, what is marriage without adultery? Look at the French! Every Frenchman of note has been cuckolded by wife or mistress: Villon, Molière, Louis XIV, Napoleon, Victor Hugo, Musset, Balzac. And why? Why, because the French really love women, that's why. Englishmen don't. That is why adultery is such a scandalous novelty in this country. I intend to set up a movement for the propagation of adultery. It will do wonders for the freedom of women. (*Pause*) My one reservation is your choice of partner. Arthur Humphreys is a walking slim volume of third-rate verse who happens to wear spectacles.

CONSTANCE But it's not your choice, is it?

OSCAR Obviously not.

CONSTANCE Anyway. It's over now. It didn't mean very much. Except attention. And I've never needed that, particularly.

OSCAR But divorce, Constance? Why divorce!

CONSTANCE It would merely define what is already there.

OSCAR No! We still have something, Constance!

CONSTANCE What? What do we have?

OSCAR (*Floundering*) The children —

CONSTANCE We three waited all day Christmas Day in this house for you. The boys were desolate. In the end I said you were — ill and couldn't come.

OSCAR I was rehearsing.

CONSTANCE Rehearsing! Rehearsing! On Christmas Day!

OSCAR I'm afraid it's the truth. Such is theatre!

CONSTANCE Actually, this is not why I asked you to come here. I have something else to tell you. I did have a visitor. On Boxing Day. Charles Brookfield.

OSCAR Brookfield? The actor? The one who plays Phipps in my play?

CONSTANCE Yes, that's the one.

OSCAR (*Nervously*) Not to complain, I hope.

CONSTANCE He sat where you are sitting now. I'm sorry to have to tell you this, Mrs Wilde —

OSCAR He's been devilishly difficult in rehearsal, Brookfield —

CONSTANCE — I knew what was coming, then. But it was the details! The details! Did he speak for an hour? I even asked questions. You know how my curiosity always gets the better of me. Even when I think I'm going to vomit.

OSCAR (*Now very nervous*) He hates me, Brookfield.

CONSTANCE Oh, yes. Indeed he does. (OSCAR *rises*) You must hear this. Sit down. (*He does*) For your own protection. He told me of that house in Little College Street. He said it was talked of among the actors. He told me of that man Taylor. Of men dressing as women. Of boys dressing as girls. He described the mock marriages between men. He described how trousers were cut to allow men to — fondle one another. He said you and Douglas frequented this place. He said, and this was his word, that you both hunted working-class men. I had this vision of a pack in a field. (*More slowly still*) Funny thing. I never questioned why he should feel free to torment me with all this. He was like a messenger in the last act of an old play.

OSCAR (*Utterly lost, an old joke dead*) What is it I once said? A man cannot be too careful in the choice of his enemies. (*She is not amused*) Sorry.

CONSTANCE Instead, I asked, is it true, Mr Brookfield, that they have their own kinds of medical problems? I mean because of what they do to one another?

OSCAR Exactly like women in other words.

CONSTANCE He said, the delicate Mr Brookfield, that he did not defile his mind by thinking of such things. And no, it is not like women.

OSCAR By God I shall kill him, Brookfield! (*Pause*) Particularly since I can't sack him from my play.

CONSTANCE I think he was quite shocked, actually, that I didn't disintegrate in tears at his feet. He is one of those men, our Mr Brookfield, who likes to cause women to suffer. So that he can then console them. I wept later, of course. Alone.

OSCAR Brookfield. What did you do with him?

CONSTANCE I ordered him out of the house.

OSCAR I am grateful that you've told me this.

CONSTANCE Then I pulled myself together. And I discovered something quite startling. I wasn't — surprised — that you were capable of — all this. No. It was as if it simply completed my knowledge of you. In a horrible kind of way, of course. You are in great danger. You know that?

OSCAR Yes.

CONSTANCE What will you do?

OSCAR Don't divorce me, Constance.

CONSTANCE I keep thinking. What is the connection? What is the connection between his foul behaviour and the beauty of what he writes? Can anyone ever answer that question?

OSCAR We are all in the gutter but some of us are looking at the stars.

CONSTANCE I think that's too easy. What I'm thinking of cannot be put in a single phrase.

OSCAR (*Unable to conceal his irritation*) Do you actually enjoy correcting me? I merely ask. You are the only person who does this, the only one!

CONSTANCE Oh, don't be so touchy, Oscar, for heavensakes. We know one another.

OSCAR What an understatement. Energy. It is all a question of energy. There is energy in the muscle. There is energy in the loop of syntax. The one feeds the other.

CONSTANCE Even when you are doing something gross?

OSCAR There is no distinction, my dear, between what is gross and what is sublime in art.

CONSTANCE (*Weeping*) And what about love? Is love gross, too?

OSCAR Ah, Constance, how I have made you suffer!

CONSTANCE And after all your protestations you're back with Douglas again —

OSCAR Yes —

CONSTANCE He's a monster, you know. It's going to destroy you.

OSCAR Yes, he is. And yes, it will. Don't divorce me, Constance, for God's sake don't —

CONSTANCE Give me one good reason why I shouldn't.

OSCAR (*Very distressed*) The children! The children! So that I may see them.

CONSTANCE Divorce. No divorce. What does it matter?

OSCAR It matters! Divorce would annihilate me! You're a long line to the shore when I'm far out at sea.

CONSTANCE When everything is in ruins you always manage to say something, Oscar, that completely stops me short.

OSCAR Don't you see what these visits mean to me? The rest of my life is madness! Madness! (*Whisper*) No divorce, then?

CONSTANCE (*Pause*) No divorce.

Music. Two of the attendants lead her off the circular space into darkness. Then, as he stands there, alone, he too is led off to the side.

CONSTANCE *sits to one side, 'reading' to the two 'children'. This shadowed image remains throughout the following speech, fading before it ends. A hanging cage is flown in. It hangs over what follows.*

The mobile staircase is pushed onto the disk once more but now reversed, with the steps hidden from the audience. The back of the staircase resembles a simple dock. Puppets of judge, lawyers and gentlemen are brought forward, crowding around the dock, waving arms. The impression is of frenzy.

WILDE *climbs the stairs and into the dock. He speaks off as if in memory.*

OSCAR   And, you, Wilde, have had the audacity to prosecute a father for libel, knowing full well that he was merely protecting his son from your foul influence. That the father was a peer of the realm, Lord Queensberry, and his son, Lord Alfred Douglas, a member of the aristocracy, simply gives some indication of the range of your upstart insolence.

You, Wilde, have been the corruptor of young men. That many of them were of the lower classes, grooms, newspaper boys, valets and the like, gives some indication of your vulgarity. That you dressed some of these youths to resemble the sons of gentlemen, putting some public school colours in their hats, elevating them above their proper sphere, gives some indication of your contempt for the ordering of society.

You, Wilde, have been a family man and the father of two children. You have violated your family and stained, beyond cleansing, the lives of your wife and children.

You, Wilde, have failed in all things. You have failed in your action against the Marquis of Queensberry. You have failed in your subversion of society. You have failed as a husband. You have failed as a father. You now have six hours and fifty minutes before the departure of the boat train from Victoria. If you have not fled this kingdom by then you will be arrested, tried. And condemned.

> *The dock/staircase is trundled off into darkness with*
> WILDE *still on it to the distant, echoing sound of*
> *the courtroom response, cheers, jeers, handclapping,*
> *various cries, insults.*
>   *Two elegant chairs are put in place on the white*
> *disk.* CONSTANCE *is led on, limping badly and sup-*
> *porting herself on a cane. She sits.* DOUGLAS, *in*
> *outdoor clothes, is conducted on behind her. He*
> *stands. At first she doesn't look at him.*

CONSTANCE If what you tell me is true, then he is doomed.

DOUGLAS But, surely, you knew all this already?

CONSTANCE They told me that the painted women of the streets danced in triumph. After the trial. Outside the Old Bailey. Is that true? Would you believe it, I even asked: Why? Silly me. Competition, I was told. There's great competition on the streets between the men and women street-walkers. Where is he now?

DOUGLAS The Cadogan Hotel. In Sloane Street.

CONSTANCE So. Your father has triumphed. They always do, don't they, fathers? And they've given him the chance to run away, have they, the authorities?

DOUGLAS Yes. He could follow all the other friends of ours into exile but he mustn't. That is why I came.

CONSTANCE I see. And did he send you here?

DOUGLAS Good Lord no!

CONSTANCE How long has he got?

DOUGLAS Three hours. He's wavering. I know it. He's wavering. There is a half-packed suitcase open on the bed. The room is like a railway station, comings and goings. Everyone screaming advice. Get the boat train, Oscar! I fled. Couldn't stand it a moment longer. Said I was going to Westminster to get help. To my cousin, George Wyndham. But what I really wanted was to come here. To you. I knew that you, of all people, would stand firm at this time.

CONSTANCE I detest the sight of you.

DOUGLAS I've changed, Constance.

CONSTANCE Indeed? Why are you trying to stop him from leaving for France?

DOUGLAS For his sake, of course!

CONSTANCE Not to prolong that absurd farce with your father?

DOUGLAS Everyone says that! Why will no one believe me? My father is a mad little man. He doesn't know it but he's only the mouthpiece, the pawn of the larger enemy. There is only one person who can fight that larger enemy. Oscar.

CONSTANCE Even if he is destroyed in the process?

DOUGLAS Yes.

CONSTANCE How very brave of you. There's no danger of *your* arrest, is there?

DOUGLAS I am in terrible danger.

CONSTANCE What's this greater enemy that you speak about?

DOUGLAS It's a body of powerful interests in this country which hates love.

CONSTANCE I see. And you know this larger enemy, do you, Lord Douglas?

DOUGLAS I was born into it, Mrs Wilde.

CONSTANCE Why did it all go so utterly wrong? Why? Oscar seemed so confident he would win.

DOUGLAS Someone betrayed us.

CONSTANCE What do you mean?

DOUGLAS Well, when we first took the case there was no doubt that we would defeat my wretched father. Everyone said that he had libelled Oscar. We were so confident that we left at once for Monte Carlo. When we got back it was all horror. Someone had given the other side, well, information. All lies, of course. But (*Shrugs*) it worked with that wretched jury.

CONSTANCE (*Pause*) Our Mr Brookfield.

DOUGLAS Who did you say?

CONSTANCE I happen to believe that information, you know. What does that make me, then? Another member of the jury?

DOUGLAS What on earth do you know about it?

CONSTANCE Oh, never mind. What is it that you want me to do for Oscar?

DOUGLAS You are the only one he will listen to!

CONSTANCE I don't trust you.

DOUGLAS I can understand that. I know what I've been like. Oscar has made me see that. He has that gift of making people see themselves. Don't you think so? That is why they hate him. Most people can't bear to look at themselves.

CONSTANCE Why! You're trying to make me share him with you!

DOUGLAS But we do that already, don't we?

CONSTANCE What can you know of me?

DOUGLAS A lot, actually. I mean I think I know you terribly well. How? Well, he never stops talking about you, for one. Used to hate it, of course. Until I listened to what he was actually saying.

CONSTANCE My life is private!

DOUGLAS You misinterpret. Never, not once, has Oscar betrayed the privacies between you two. What he does talk about, endlessly I have to say, is your capacity to — accept.

CONSTANCE Of course. Accept! In that way I may be abused, humiliated!

DOUGLAS Oh, do let's stop talking about ourselves! This is infinitely bigger than any one person. How Oscar conducts himself now will determine the future of many, many people. Many of them frightened little people in lonely rooms. They will see him stand his ground. And his example will give them hope. Only Oscar is capable of that because of the immense hate that he has provoked.

CONSTANCE You sound extraordinarily disinterested, Lord Douglas. Well, I'm not. I'm only interested now in the survival of my two boys. For that, I want him as far away as possible. At the very least, the South of France.

DOUGLAS Constance, Constance! You don't know what you're condemning him to. I do. You don't know the deathly life of the invert in exile. I do. I know it so well. Imprisonment in a villa above Monte Carlo with the likes of Podge Somerset. The perpetual whine, the perpetual, futile plans to return home. Capri, Taormina, Tangiers. Splendid to visit, but what if there were nothing else? Ever? Oscar would go insane. Apart at all from the fact that he would see it as cowardice.

CONSTANCE You'd prefer him to be a victim?

DOUGLAS I'd prefer him to be Oscar.

CONSTANCE Perhaps I have underestimated you.

DOUGLAS I have never threatened you. Oscar says that, you know. He says, at some level she is never threatened.

CONSTANCE No, not threatened. Hurt, yes.

DOUGLAS Well, then. We can have an understanding, can we not?

CONSTANCE There's something about sexuality that raises a primitive fear in people. I've never felt that. And that is why I hate hypocrisy and all the dangerous, malevolent hypocrites sitting in high places. Tell him I said he should fight them! Fight them! Fight them to the bitter end.

DOUGLAS (*Producing paper and pencil*) Would you write a short letter to him?

CONSTANCE A letter!

DOUGLAS Yes, you know how Oscar adores letters. (*She takes the paper and pencil and writes*) It would mean so much to him to read your actual words. There is only one thing he prefers to receiving letters. That is, tearing up the bad ones.

CONSTANCE (*Handing him the note*) You may read it if you wish.

DOUGLAS I *always* read other people's letters. (*Reading*) 'Dear Oscar. Fight them to the end. Constance.' I feel as if I'm carrying a last-minute reprieve to the gallows.

CONSTANCE Well, then, you should hurry along, shouldn't you? (*He turns to go*) I want him to read that before he leaves that room.

> *He looks at her as she steps off the circle. Then he steps off and they stand to one side in darkness, watching.*
> *A loud sound of clappers as the attendants lead* OSCAR *on to the centre of the circle. He is wearing a fur overcoat and top-hat. His costume is such that it will come apart in pieces during what follows. As he speaks the attendants crouch at his feet, like dogs.*

OSCAR Certain melodramas rise to the Aristotelian, others

descend to the depths of realism. Mine was somewhere in between. The policeman's knock on the door. The heavy hand on one's shoulder.

(*Outburst*) Where is Bosie? Why isn't he here? Room Number 53, the Cadogan Hotel. My rather vulgar Upper Room. From now on my fate would be determined by numbers.

Why do all these people keep urging me to go abroad? It is deafening. I have just *been* abroad. One cannot keep going abroad. Unless one is a missionary. Or a commercial traveller. That sounded so much better the first time round.

The boat train departed from Victoria at 5.45 p.m. The knock on the door came exactly at ten minutes past six. They wished me to cut and run, you see. Mr Wilde, I presume? Yes? I must ask you, sir, to accompany me to the police station. Decent opening lines, no?

When the policeman finally confronts his quarry there is always this exchange between equals. A sort of civility that can only be born out of a shared familiarity with transgression. My coppers. Inspector Richards with his warts, his doleful sergeant holding on to a scrap of paper for dear life. Splendid fellows, those two!

(*Anguish*) Why isn't Bosie back? For God's sake go and find him, someone! I wrote to Constance. Told her to — protect the children. Lock the house. I told her that no one should have access to my study but the servants. Perhaps I was thinking that only servants should read what I had written from this day out?

(*Great cry*) Bosie! He has abandoned me! He wasn't up to it when the chips were down. Funk! Well, my dear, cheers! Why am I not running away? They do not understand, you see, that it was long past all that. I was already condemned. I was already in that filthy cell, stinking of diarrhoea and the smell of every inmate who had ever been there down the endless years. The Community of Man, oh, yes, indeed. I was already staggering on the treadmill, I was already turning the crank, my daily duty. When men set out to destroy their own kind they give them tasks of exquisite uselessness.

I already knew all this before I put on my top-coat with my two coppers in tow. I knew the future. I knew the past. I knew what it was to be among the olives in that garden at even-tide, the fake kiss, the hysterical disciples and the violent sacrifice of the one for the many.

> *The cage is lowered. A piercing cacophony of sound and discordant notes, canned laughter and applause, night-screams and cries of agony and, as a bass tone, endless opening and banging shut of prison cell doors, feet shuffling along stone corridors, indecipherable shouts of command.*
>
> *The attendants have leaped upon* OSCAR, *tearing at his clothes and hair. The clothes come apart in strips, the hair comes off in tufts. He is dragged, half-naked, half-mutilated, back to the cage which is now the only thing on stage that is lit. He is pushed naked into the cage, and it swings aloft. In there, he is hosed down by the attendants.*
>
> CONSTANCE *and* DOUGLAS *watch all this in silhouette, backs to audience. Lights down on all but* CONSTANCE. *She turns to the audience walking well downstage.*

CONSTANCE It was as if I married him a second time in that disgusting prison but this time not the bride in cowslip yellow crowned with myrtle in St James's Church, oh no, this time naked in the bed of filth. You see, I saw Papa, too, in that cage, degraded, loving, generous, reviled, monstrous Papa. I loved two criminals, you see. Papa-Oscar. Oscar-Papa. And he said to me, from that cage, nothing can be concealed here, Constance, poor, naked wretches, nothing to cover them, no words, no love.

People keep asking me questions: What will you

do now, Constance? And what will you tell the children?

She stands there as the lights come down.

PART TWO

Music: Organ, variations on the Missa in Commemoratione Omnium Fidelium Defunctorum. *Rising and falling through the following:* CONSTANCE *is still standing where she was at the end of Part One, still facing the audience. The iron cage has been pushed forward, downstage. The white disk hangs above it, a large moon or gigantic wafer. There is a hidden ramp behind the cage, beneath the disk.*

OSCAR *is in the cage, bedraggled prison uniform, a worn, beaten figure on his knees, praying, back to audience. One ear is bandaged with a filthy cloth.*

CONSTANCE The children! The children! he cried. The children! And I remembered how one day on the beach at Brighton I was alone on a deckchair, the children at my feet among the sandcastles. And suddenly this large figure appeared in the distance in inappropriate black, it being high summer, the hot sun — flapping like a monstrous bird. It was Oscar. He ran across the strand, waving his arms so that I thought something quite dreadful had happened. The children! he cried. The children! Tears streaming down his face. Are they all right? Yes, of course they're all right, I said. Oh, my God, he cried, collapsing on the sand beside me. I was asleep and dreamt that they had been swept out to sea!

Pause.

That, too, you see, is Oscar. The other question people keep asking me is: (*Voice*) You saw him in prison, Constance, what was it really like? Was it

49

really so very dreadful? (*Self again*) They make it sound like a slightly disagreeable tea-party. I cannot raise my left arm anymore. Did I really fly? Or was I cast down?

(*Voice*) What did he look like, Constance? Did he have to wear those awful duds, the ones with those funny arrows? (*Self again*) Actually — I said to them in my best nonchalant, wife-of-a-celebrity voice — Christ came to him in his cell. That stopped them in their tracks, I can tell you. Always managed to have the best of company, our Oscar. Wherever he found himself.

(*Shrill, deep distress*) Dirt, they said, dirt — he is dirt, stained bed-linen, well, then, stick him in the dirt, rub his face in it, diarrhoea and urine. Christ came in the dirt, obvious, isn't it? I followed him! Followed him down into the dirt. And loved him there in my bowels. Human, indeed!

> *She turns and watches what follows. The six attendants, in black chasubles, white gloves, lead on* DOUGLAS *in procession, along the ramp, beneath the white disk, above* OSCAR's *head.* DOUGLAS *is dressed in the full black, traditional vestments of the Mass of the Dead, chasuble, stole, cincture etc.*
>
> *Two of the attendants carry tall, black-stemmed, altar candlesticks with lit candles. A third carries a large display of lily-of-the-valley and ciborium, a fourth, the large, traditional Mass missal. This is held open before* DOUGLAS, *resting on the attendant's head so that* DOUGLAS, *as priest, may read from it.*
>
> *The total effect is of a fantastic dream or nightmare.*

DOUGLAS (*Intoning, hands outstretched*) Requiem aeternam dona eis, Domine: et lux perpetua luceat eis. In memoria aeterna erit iustus, ab auditione mala non timebit.

Absolve, Domine, animas omnium fidelium defunctorum ab omni vinculo delictorum. Et lucis aeternae beatitudine perfrui.

A massed male choir breaks out into the opening verses of the Dies Irae *and it runs through the following: the attendants strip* DOUGLAS *of the outer vestments so that he is now a Christ-like figure in long white alb. One of them hands him the ciborium. They conduct him down into the cage where he gives communion from the ciborium to a reverential* OSCAR. *The attendants take the ciborium from* DOUGLAS. *OSCAR kisses* DOUGLAS *on each of his proferred palms, prostrates himself and kisses his feet.* DOUGLAS *raises* OSCAR *and kisses him on the mouth. At this the attendants applaud noisily and sweep* DOUGLAS *away, out, up and across the ramp into darkness while the choral singing is sharply cut off.*

OSCAR (*On his knees*) Domine, non sum dignus! Domine, non sum dignus!

Sound: marching along prison corridors, steel doors swinging open, banged shut. A second cage is moved in beside the first. CONSTANCE *is conducted into this. Puppet gaolers. The other attendants stand to either side, guards or macabre waiters. One of them takes a piece of paper from* CONSTANCE *and carries it to* OSCAR.

CONSTANCE (*Cry*) Why will you not let me touch him? (*Rising, holding the bars of her cage*)

OSCAR (*Reading, voice breaking*) It says here that she simply turned her face to the wall and died. Just like that. Oh, my God, poor Mama! Is this my brother's handwriting?

CONSTANCE Yes.

OSCAR Still trying to write lurid journalism, that brother of mine. You know she came to me, Mother, as an apparition in the cell but she didn't speak.

CONSTANCE I wanted to be the one to tell you, Oscar. About her death.

OSCAR Thank you. Do you know, I was always amazed at how close you two were.

CONSTANCE She was a deeply serious person, your mother. Underneath those outlandish clothes. (*Pause*) Can you still not eat the food they give you?

OSCAR I eat the soup. And a little bread.

CONSTANCE How is your ear infection?

OSCAR It has stopped draining. I think.

CONSTANCE (*Cry: to* ATTENDANTS) Please! Let me touch him!

OSCAR Don't, Constance. They punish each indiscretion. I would get solitary for three days. I cannot bear it anymore. Oh, Mama, Mama, what have I done to you!

CONSTANCE You've suffered enough, Oscar.

OSCAR I cannot suffer enough.

CONSTANCE Why, that's simply not true.

OSCAR (*Hard laugh*) Constance still correcting me! Sorry. Didn't mean that. Joke.

CONSTANCE I was simply thinking of the great courage you always have.

OSCAR Had. Past tense. She never lost her dignity, you know, Mother. Even when she was down on her uppers. Not a brass farthing in the house. Alone in that darkened room waiting to die. Couldn't bear to let people see her poverty. She was always capable of the right gesture. Even with that monster, my father. Do you know, when he was dying she conducted one of his mistresses to the bedside and left them alone together. She belonged to a future. A future that may never materialize, alas.

CONSTANCE There's another reason that I came.

OSCAR (*New anxiety*) Is it the boys? Has something happened to them? Are they safe?

CONSTANCE Yes — yes — yes — they're perfectly fine.

OSCAR (*Pause*) Constance. (*Pause*) What have you told them? About me?

CONSTANCE I say that you are away on a long journey.

OSCAR But there was something else, why you came.

CONSTANCE (*Distress*) I came to confess.

OSCAR To what?

CONSTANCE Confess! Confess! (*Very distressed*) I kept saying to myself — throughout all the horrors — I kept saying, remember, remember, it's all human, Constance! Human! That way I could somehow accept it all. (*Bitter*) Constance's great capacity to accept everything. Then one day, I don't know why, I don't even remember when — I saw this for what it was. Flattery. I was simply flattering myself with my own — (*Contempt*) goodness —

OSCAR Constance —

CONSTANCE No, hear me out. Suddenly there was nothing between me and absolute horror, something monstrous within me, some squat creature. It was terrifying.

OSCAR But why are you telling me all this now?

CONSTANCE Because it has to do with you.

OSCAR How with me?

CONSTANCE Don't know, really. I mean I detest the life you've been living. I find it utterly disgusting. And yet I know that this facing myself or whatever it is, exposure or something, has to do with the way you've exposed yourself. Isn't that strange? I felt so utterly secure when I first met you, all that brilliant camouflage, all that masking. And now that you've broken I am broken, too. Very odd, actually.

OSCAR It takes great suffering to see that.

CONSTANCE Oh, it's not a bit grandiose like that. It's infinitely more mundane. Actually quite ugly, as a matter of fact. One day in Genoa it was. The pain from my spine particularly severe. One minute I was crouching there, unable to straighten up. But congratulating myself. Of course! Bravo Constance! You can do it, there's a good girl. Put up with anything. Yes, you can! Next moment I straightened up in unimaginable pain, my mouth screaming out the most frightful obscenities. At myself. At you. Gross words I didn't know I possessed. Spewing out of me. Like a sewer. I believe I blasphemed. Yes! I certainly swore at God for this thing called existence. I felt utterly degraded. The funny thing is I also felt somehow — exhilarated. All at the same time.

OSCAR It is Christ!

CONSTANCE I beg your pardon!

OSCAR When he said: Forgive thine enemy, it wasn't for the relief of the enemy, it was for the healing of oneself. Oh, Constance, I've learned so much in here! We are born to live with contradiction. I used to hold contradiction in a single phrase. Now I am learning to hold contradiction in my heart. Everything in this life threatens to contradict something else.

CONSTANCE As man and woman.

OSCAR That too, that too.

CONSTANCE I love you, Oscar, the way you once said you loved me. Remember? That day in Dublin, in Merrion Square?

OSCAR (*Eagerly*) You mean we can be together again with the two boys!

CONSTANCE They miss you frightfully.

OSCAR Please tell me more about the two of them, Constance. What do they do each day?

CONSTANCE Well, Cyril still wants to be a sailor. Royal Navy. He's got lots of books about it. Practises his salute in front of the mirror. Terribly brave. Each day we must spin the globe and sail all around the world. That makes me feel young again.

OSCAR And Vyvie?

CONSTANCE Oh, he's very imaginative, actually. Makes things with bits of coloured paper. But he keeps asking: Where are my tin soldiers, Mummy? Do you know all the children's toys fetched thirty shillings at the auction?

OSCAR Thirty pieces of silver. Where have I heard that before! (*Pause*) I did all that!

CONSTANCE You are not responsible for the evil of other people, Oscar.

OSCAR I gave them licence.

CONSTANCE Our splendid civilization has given them licence, Oscar. (*Pause*) When you waited in the hotel. Before your arrest. Did you receive a letter from me?

OSCAR No. What was in it?

CONSTANCE I told you not to run away.

OSCAR Oh, if only I had received it —

54

CONSTANCE I gave it to Douglas —

OSCAR I see. (*Pause*) I'm afraid he is particularly irresponsible in the matter of correspondence. Something to do with public schooling, I believe.

CONSTANCE Oscar. Have you finished with him?

OSCAR I was mad, Constance. For four whole years, I was out of my mind. Didn't you see it? I see it now with the most awful clarity.

CONSTANCE (*Whisper*) What about Douglas?

OSCAR He is trying to sell my letters, you know. Can you believe it! He is offering his story for money to newspapers! But no one wants anything to do with him.

CONSTANCE (*Almost breaking*) What about you and Douglas?

OSCAR If he were here this instant I'd kill him. They talk about my crime. Ha! My only crime is that I made a god out of common clay. That is unforgivable.

CONSTANCE (*Scream*) Answer me!

> Blare of music. CONSTANCE's cage is thrown open and she is led out. The cage is quickly taken off while OSCAR, sunken, remains in his own cage.
>
> DOUGLAS, in long travelling coat, white hat and cane appears upstage in a bright spot.
>
> A frenzied movement: attendants with puppets of travellers, complete with suitcases, valises, portmanteaus. Rushing train sounds. Engine smoke. DOUGLAS is swept up in this travel. CONSTANCE, in travelling coat and hat, with the two child puppets, travelling in a cut-away railway carriage which heaves and shudders to loud train noise and reeling, flashing light. Train comes to a halt. Attendant/porters conduct CONSTANCE and her luggage off the carriage. An hotel entrance. Hôtel de la Gare. CONSTANCE and the children are turned away from the hotel door by an attendant/hotel manager and attendant/doorman.
>
> Back in the carriage once more. Repeat of the shuddering journey, train whistle. Again the journey comes to a halt. Silence. A dazed CONSTANCE is brought forward. The child puppets and her travelling coat

and hat are removed. A white garden seat is placed for her but first she addresses the audience. DOUGLAS *finishes his travelling, coat and hat off.*

CONSTANCE Somewhere between Switzerland and the Italian plain I knew he would never answer me. I decided to change our name. Never again could we call ourselves Wilde. It was an ending but not *the* ending. You see I hadn't confessed all to him. I was unable to. And there could be no ending until I did so. Confess. Secret. To fall again. (*Pauses, glances off*) Who is it? Who is that? (*She turns in shock.* DOUGLAS *steps forward and they are lit in bright sunlight*) How did you know where I was?

DOUGLAS Why are we both living abroad? Hm? Apart from the insufferably dull world of commerce, there are only two reasons why people travel. Culture and criminality. You and I are abroad for the same reason. His name is Oscar, the cultured criminal. Our circuits may be different, true. I may fancy Capri with odd diversions to Monte Carlo to play the tables at the Casino. Or Sicily with odd diversions to Algiers for the Arabs. While you move from Germany to Switzerland to Monaco to Italy, hobnobbing, I believe, with the Ranee of Sarawak and Princess Alice of Monaco.

CONSTANCE Why are you here?

DOUGLAS (*Pauses*) To settle our differences.

CONSTANCE (*Impatience*) We are utterly different.

DOUGLAS My dear, in your desperate need to have everything black and white, you utterly miss the point.

CONSTANCE Oh? Really? And what might that be, may I ask?

DOUGLAS That there are no absolutes except in the desperate imagination of men and women. No black. No white. No good. No evil. No male. No female. Everything runs together and runs in and out of everything else. But human beings cannot abide such glorious confusion. So, they invent what is called morality to keep everyone and everything in place. I am quoting, I believe, from the testament of the beloved apostle,

St Oscar.

CONSTANCE   (*Cry*) Oscar has changed. I know it. I've seen him in prison. What's more, he is contemptuous of you. (DOUGLAS *laughs*) Why do you laugh?

DOUGLAS   Why do I ever laugh? Oh, Oscar, Oscar!

CONSTANCE   You *mock* him!

DOUGLAS   (*Fiercely, complete change in tone*) I *know* him! And he knows me. He has taught me everything I know. Everything! Like most aristocrats I was raised in boorishness. He taught me that anything unearned is not only without value, it is the source of corruption. He taught me that we must learn our true nature and be true to that or else we are damned. He taught me to live when I was merely breathing. He taught me to love. What every human creature may have. If she has the courage, that is.

CONSTANCE   I see. That is quite extraordinary. Somehow I always thought of you as superficial. I was wrong, obviously.

DOUGLAS   You see! We *can* be friends.

CONSTANCE   Don't talk nonsense, please! I shouldn't allow you near me, if I could help it. All you've done is convince me that whatever it is between you and Oscar, well, it's substantial, if nothing else. And, therefore, my relationship with him becomes that much less. That's all.

DOUGLAS   You talk like a clerk. Adding up. One column on one side, one on the other.

CONSTANCE   That's the only way you can understand it, isn't it? Do you realize, Lord Douglas, how essentially vulgar you are?

DOUGLAS   My! My! Vulgar now, are we?

CONSTANCE   Get out of my — home!

DOUGLAS   And tantrums, too! Heavens!

CONSTANCE   At once! Do you want me to call someone to eject you? Do you?

DOUGLAS   Just a moment. Before I leave. May I see the two boys?

CONSTANCE   (*A long, long pause while she studies him in growing fury*) What did you say?

DOUGLAS   What? What?

CONSTANCE   Get out of here!

DOUGLAS What is it now?

CONSTANCE Out! Out!

DOUGLAS You're — sick!

CONSTANCE (*Shrill*) Why have you asked to see the two boys?

DOUGLAS To say hello. Goodbye.

CONSTANCE Why — why — why?

DOUGLAS (*Almost speechless*) Oscar's children —

CONSTANCE *My* children!

DOUGLAS That is incontestible. What is going on here?

CONSTANCE (*Trying to calm herself*) Why did you ask to see the children?

DOUGLAS Why do *you* think I wish to see them, Constance? Yes. Why? Go on. Do tell me.

CONSTANCE (*Sudden, total calm*) They are safe.

DOUGLAS Safe from what?

CONSTANCE From all that — filth!

DOUGLAS (*Fury*) Filth is it? The only filth, madam, is what is presently in your own mind. How dare you make such insinuations. Typical, how typical of you women. Tight, tight!

CONSTANCE (*Lost in her own thought*) Protected —

DOUGLAS But I'm not going to let this pass. No! You've made a dreadful insinuation against me. I would never harm a child. Never! What gives you the right? To imply such things?

CONSTANCE If Oscar were here he would —

DOUGLAS If Oscar were here he would be pleased that I admire the beauty of his sons. Very simple. Very pure.

CONSTANCE He would physically eject you if he were here! He has turned his back on your kind.

DOUGLAS Oscar is positively surrounded, my dear, with, as you put it, my kind. We call them the sorority of St Mary Magdalen. Robbie Ross, Reggie Turner, More Adey. The wonder is how they find room for all of them in that cell of his. What a crush!

CONSTANCE Not true — not true —

DOUGLAS He is incapable of wiping his nose without their advice. Why, they have even succeeded in turning him against me. The little —

CONSTANCE (*Whisper*) It's not true!

DOUGLAS I'm afraid it is, my dear.

CONSTANCE I know an Oscar that no one else can know!

DOUGLAS Precisely. There are many Oscars. That is what makes him so seductive.

CONSTANCE But I spoke to him in prison —

DOUGLAS Prison is one thing, freedom is another. Besides, he is now about to re-emerge, I believe, like that other beloved one, from the tomb.

CONSTANCE He has lied to me again! Lied to me!

DOUGLAS My dear, you mustn't distress yourself. You know it's not lying. It's just that Oscar has to re-invent everything as he goes along. One simply has to work around his creativity.

CONSTANCE (*Utterly lost*) We both said that it would be the same as before.

DOUGLAS Nothing, my dear, *nothing* is ever the same as before. That is my lesson for the day. (*Whirling away*)

CONSTANCE (*Screaming after him*) Why should I believe you, of all people?

> She stands a moment and then walks off.
> Music. A great peal, a hallelujah. The attendants use their clappers loudly. Two of them lead OSCAR out of his cage, into the light.
> Chairs on the white disk, OSCAR is now seated on it and given a drink by the attendants. DOUGLAS comes forward and is just about to step onto the disk when an attendant touches his arm and hands him a letter. He holds it up to the light, searching its contents. No good. Looks about and then delicately prises open the envelope and takes out the letter. CONSTANCE stands to one side in a fading light. She speaks, as DOUGLAS reads silently, the light gradually going down on her as he takes over.

CONSTANCE 'Dear Oscar, It is so difficult for me, but I am trying to understand, to forgive. That's what is important, isn't it? To forgive? The only hope for us is that we close the door on the past. Can you do that, Oscar? Can you?'

DOUGLAS (*Reading*) 'In particular, I must insist that you never see Lord Alfred Douglas again' — (*He carefully refolds the letter, puts it back in the envelope, reseals and hands it to attendant*) See that Mr Wilde gets that, would you? In about three weeks time. (*Aside to* AUDIENCE) The whole history of our dramatic literature is dependent upon the inadequacies of the postal service. (*Steps onto the disk: to* WILDE) I'm here!

OSCAR Bosie! I've been thinking. But when you visited with her that time, what exactly did she say to you? About my seeing the boys again? What were her exact words?

DOUGLAS Never! Never!

OSCAR Never! Oh, what a word! My two boys! Never!

DOUGLAS Do let's forget about her, darling. It's such a bore —

OSCAR I simply cannot understand it. Her letters to me have been so — warm. And now, this silence.

DOUGLAS But *I'm* here now, darling —

OSCAR It's been worse than prison, waiting here in Berneval. Oh dear boy, you've no idea what excruciating tortures they devise for one at the lesser French seaside resorts — table d'hôte with the English spinsters at six, dominoes and spittle with the village elders by the quayside —

DOUGLAS But what about *me*!

OSCAR (*Looks at him for a moment*) Oh, dear sweet, beautiful boy! Hush! I'd be suicidal if you hadn't come, you know that.

DOUGLAS But do I? You spend every waking hour talking about her.

OSCAR You're being cruel again, Bosie —

DOUGLAS It's a pain in the neck, that's what it is! It's like living in a ghastly domestic novel in three volumes.

> OSCAR *laughs, a bit forced, and clicks his fingers at an attendant who promptly produces more drinks, the perfect waiter.*

OSCAR You adorable boy! My goodness, we are going to have such fun — I am so happy, Bosie — How

I've missed your — sharpness, your — attack! Let's demolish everyone and everything!

DOUGLAS   Let's begin by forgetting this family of yours, shall we?

OSCAR   But you said yourself you'd love to have the boys come and visit —

DOUGLAS   (*Pause*) Yes. (*Pause*) No!

OSCAR   We could take them boating and swimming. Cyril is terrifically athletic, you know —

DOUGLAS   (*A savage turn: outburst*) What utter nonsense!

OSCAR   May take time, of course. But I know Constance. She moves slowly and now that she is away from sniggering, malevolent England —

DOUGLAS   (*Fury*) I'm not talking about her! I'm talking about us!

OSCAR   Why are you so angry?

DOUGLAS   Who do you think we are? Some kind of holy family? We are outside the law, my friend. We trawl the streets. We pick fruit where we can.

OSCAR   I hate this cynicism in you, Bosie! Hate it! It demeans you — I will not be brutalized! They tried that. Every conceivable disgusting way, they tried. And failed —

DOUGLAS   Allow me to make a list for you. Your marriage has ended. You are extremely lucky that your wife continues your allowance, paltry as it is, subject to good behaviour. You are an ex-con. You are extremely lucky that your lover finds you — irresistible. You are a permanent exile. You are extremely lucky that police procedures are as variable as the European climate. (*Clincher*) And your boys are gone. Forever.

OSCAR   Why are you doing this to me, Bosie!

DOUGLAS   Truth.

OSCAR   I've spent a lifetime expressing the truth.

DOUGLAS   Indeed. But always in the most delightfully ambivalent fashion.

OSCAR   You abuse me!

DOUGLAS   Don't whinge, Oscar. I detest whingeing.

OSCAR   You're so cold, cold —

OSCAR *is still in the chair.* DOUGLAS *goes behind*

him, taking him, fiercely, by the hair, pulling the head back, sharply, exposing the throat. OSCAR *is completely passive throughout all this, face up.*

DOUGLAS (*A full-tongued kiss*) But you love my coldness, don't you, my love? You find it intensely — satisfying. You said so yourself. (*Each single word tasted*) Marble. Muscle. (*Again, the tongued kiss*) I love your mouth. Mouth. It is as if all the senses of your body were drawn into this single organ. What a mouth you have, Oscar! Have you ever thought? This is where your real genius resides. Mouth. This is where your soul is. Soul. Hole. Tongue. Lick. (*Another tongued kiss*) La vipère rouge. When your mouth opens, I would go in, in, in. Swallow. More than any other kiss, I love the kiss of betrayal.

CONSTANCE *crosses the stage at the back, walking with difficulty, holding the child puppets, in sailor suits, by the hands. Suddenly the puppeteers whisk the puppets away in a wild, childish run and then they are gone.*

CONSTANCE (*Turns to audience*) They keep running away from me and I cannot follow. They see it as a game. Mummy cannot run! Mummy cannot — The other day I overheard them. Behind the orange tree. Whispering. About him. He might as well be dead, Cyril said. Vyvie wept. I couldn't move towards them. The pain in my back became so bad that I cried out. I heard this sort of braying come from my mouth. They came around the orange tree, two very dusty little boys. I said sometimes one's Papa can be cruel. I don't care, Cyril said. Was your Papa cruel, Mummy, Vyvie asked? I shook and shook as if I were perishing in that perfect sunshine. Standing there. We three in silence. (*Pause*) He never answered my last letter. Weeks passed. Not a word from him. Then I realised that there was nothing left. Except my need to confess.

She walks back into darkness. She will now be dressed exactly as in the opening of the play, with a cane. DOUGLAS *breaks away from* OSCAR.

DOUGLAS Do we have any more cash?

OSCAR You mean you've spent the rest of it? All of it? On what? Those little boy bitches down on the water-front?

DOUGLAS Now — now! Now — now!

OSCAR You've spent our last bloody penny —

DOUGLAS But where's all this other money you were promised?

OSCAR Is that the only reason you have stayed with me? Money?

DOUGLAS You said my darling mother was to give you two hundred quid —

OSCAR Indeed. Provided I stay away from you.

DOUGLAS Oh, Mother, Mother, you excel yourself. What about all those bucks you were to make from the land of Uncle Sam? Wasn't that well-known pornographer Smithers going to make your fortune for you? America awaits your great poem, Mr Wilde.

OSCAR It hasn't — happened —

DOUGLAS I see. Of course, if you'd played your cards right with that wife of yours —

OSCAR Played my cards! Played my cards!

DOUGLAS — she wouldn't have withdrawn that damned allowance, such as it was!

OSCAR Played my cards! How vulgar!

DOUGLAS You're such a snob, Oscar! It's laughable — Enter the Duchess! It doesn't wash, dearie, not with me, luv, it don't.

OSCAR You're despicable.

DOUGLAS Of course. How predictable! I'm despicable. Do you know, your snobbery has brought us to this?

OSCAR What rubbish!

DOUGLAS That actor. Brookfield. Remember? How he gathered the dirt on us, so to speak. And why? Because you humiliated him. I heard about it. One should not wear gloves during afternoon tea, Brookfield. That's what you said to him. In public! And in America, of all places! You committed the cardinal sin. You corrected an Englishman in a matter of etiquette. One never does that. Particularly if one is not English oneself. Particularly if he is an actor and trained to imitate his betters.

He clicks his fingers. The attendants come forward with a cape and hat. One of the attendants will also offer him a smart travelling bag.

OSCAR Poor Brookfield! What are you doing?
DOUGLAS Dressing.
OSCAR But why?
DOUGLAS One always dresses properly for the outdoors.
OSCAR Why are you leaving?
DOUGLAS There is nothing left here. Is there?
OSCAR Oh, Bosie! Bosie!
DOUGLAS Oh — Oscar — Oscar — (*He comes up beside* OSCAR. OSCAR *lifts a hand towards him but* DOUGLAS *brushes it aside*) The truth is, m'dear, you are only of interest when you are on a pedestal —

DOUGLAS *steps off the disk, leaving* OSCAR *slumped behind him. He seems to be about to leave but then returns and addresses the audience directly.* CONSTANCE *steps out of the darkness.*

You're wondering, aren't you? How it all ended? Not him. We all know what happened to him on the streets of Paris. No, not him, her! Well, she died. The pain became excruciating. She made the mistake of entering an Italian clinic and like many another who did so she never came out again. I liked her, really liked her. If only we had met at another time, another place. Pity. Because, you see, when it all ended I felt as if I had been released from a malevolent white circle. Free at last! And I outlived them both. By nearly half a century, as a matter of fact. Married, settled down. Dabbled in the horses, bit of shooting here and there. Perfectly normal human being once more. Not like that dreadful little shit I used to be. Absolutely not. No. Normal! Normal! Normal!

He walks back and off into the darkness. The atten-dants come and dress OSCAR *in hat and cloak and hand him a cane.* CONSTANCE *and* OSCAR *are now in exactly the same scene as in the opening of the play but on the forestage, not the white disk.*

The attendants have rolled off the white disk hang-ing it stage left. Beneath it they set up an outdoor Parisian café scene.

CONSTANCE No! No! No!

OSCAR I must see them, Constance, must, must. They're my children too.

CONSTANCE I've never denied that — that's not what this is about!

OSCAR Well? What is it about then?

CONSTANCE (*Pause*) Confession.

OSCAR Confession?

CONSTANCE You know, he said to me that you had the gift to make others see themselves.

OSCAR Who said that?

CONSTANCE Douglas.

OSCAR Bosie! What a burden I placed upon him! And one so young. I wonder what will become of him now?

CONSTANCE I didn't quite know what he meant, then. I know now.

OSCAR (*Pause*) Your fall. Why you fell.

CONSTANCE Yes.

OSCAR But something else?

CONSTANCE On the landing —

OSCAR What did you see, Constance?

CONSTANCE (*Low*) Unspeakable —

OSCAR I am here, Constance —

CONSTANCE You are here, Oscar. Then I am not alone.

OSCAR No. You are not alone.

CONSTANCE Then, at last, I am able to face it.

OSCAR What was it, Constance?

CONSTANCE Can't be told. Can only be — acted out. Little girl. On the stairs. Waiting for Papa to come home. Papa came

65

home early. Always early. He gave me gifts. On the landing. (*Girlishly*) What is it, Papa? Me, please! Me, please! Ribbons. Paper, gorgeous paper — show! Love-touch — secret — secret — fall —

She drops to her knees. A great, thumping beat of sound. We watch as OSCAR *watches and the attendants bring on a gigantic puppet: Victorian gentleman, red cheeks, black moustache, bowler hat, umbrella, frock-coat. Bright paper package dangling from one puppet arm.*

The procession reaches CONSTANCE *and the puppet is made to squat or kneel before her, it and the attendants blocking her from view. The whole group heaves and humps several times and* OSCAR *turns away in distress. Then the attendants, very quickly, carry off the puppet, a lifeless thing, and we see* CONSTANCE, *retching, on her knees.* OSCAR *tries to reach out to her but she gestures him away.*

OSCAR Constance — !

CONSTANCE I have loved evil! I have loved evil!

OSCAR No, Constance! No!

CONSTANCE You said to me, you're different, Constance. Remember? That long ago afternoon in Merrion Square? You're uncontaminated by life, Constance. That's what you said. What utter rot! You needed to invent me because you couldn't face life as it really is. Uncontaminated! How more contaminated could I be?

OSCAR (*Cry of pain*) You were but a child! An innocent child!

CONSTANCE Child — children! You — I. All connected. Everything connected. You know I was unable to face that — thing without you being by my side? Isn't that remarkable? I used to think: nothing can touch me, married to this brilliant, outrageous man! I am safe beneath this glittering surface! Whereas the truth was you were drawing me into horror, step by step, like a dangerous guide, the horror of myself. You have made me brave, Oscar. And now that it is all out our marriage has finally and utterly ended. Odd, isn't it? All that remains now are the two children.

OSCAR (*Last ditch effort*) I must see them before I die!

CONSTANCE (*Weeping*) No black. No white. No right, no wrong! No male, no female! That's what you believe, isn't it? You and Douglas? Everything in confusion! How wrong you are!

OSCAR You're simply disturbed, Constance, confused. That horrible man — your father!

CONSTANCE Confused? Confused! I'm absolutely and totally clear. I'm clear enough to draw a line and say that's it. Are you? Can you draw a line even if it cuts you in two? Can you? Do you know what it costs me? To deny my children their own father? Do you? It's like bleeding inside!

OSCAR It has to do with your suffering as a child!

CONSTANCE It has nothing to do with suffering. It has to do with definition!

OSCAR You've even changed their name! Not Wilde any more.

CONSTANCE They and I have to live in the real world.

OSCAR What is the real world?

CONSTANCE Oh my God, you have learned nothing! Nothing!

OSCAR I've learned what it is that separates us. (*Breaks*) Cyril is the one I worry about most. He is such a perfectionist that he may do something terrible with his life! (*Pause*) Constance, I am still their father —

CONSTANCE And what does that mean?

OSCAR (*More uncertainly*) Duty —

CONSTANCE The only duty of a parent is to make childhood possible. For as long as possible. But you haven't an inkling of what that means.

OSCAR No? Perhaps not. Perhaps you are right. Perhaps you are wrong. Perhaps. But you will never tolerate the world of perhaps, will you, Constance? (*Pause*) There is one final thing I must ask of you.

CONSTANCE What is it?

OSCAR I want you to think of me as — (*Pause*) Will you be my sister now, Constance? (*She nods her head dumbly, beyond words*) I will go back to the streets of Paris,

67

then. I'm like a monument now, you know. I sit, daily, on the pavement outside the Café de Flore. They allow me to sit there, you see, with saucer and empty cup. A monument. What am I waiting for? A few francs? The end of the century? The fall of night? Do you know, I dread the thought of living beyond the century. The very thought of putting nineteen hundred and something atop one's notepaper gives one the willies! And yet! There are times when I see the mist of the future lift. I see them there, in rows, standing. And, you know something? They are applauding me —

He turns and leaves her and disappears from view. She still stands there, her eyes still closed. As she speaks, two attendants, figures of death, gather close about her, one pushing a surgical trolley, another carrying a white sheet.

At the same time, lights up on the Paris street scene: the figure of OSCAR, *long cloak, long hair, wide black hat, seated at the outdoor café table, back to audience.*

CONSTANCE 'Dearest Cyril, Dearest Vyvyan, my two darling boys, I am writing this letter because tomorrow I must go into the clinic at Genoa. Please don't be frightened. I am — (*Pause, going on with difficulty*) They are going to — it's just a matter, really, of taking away Mummy's pain. That's good, isn't it? I wanted to write about your father. All his troubles arose from his own father, from the way his father crushed something within the soul of his own son. But your father is a great man. He had this terrible, strange vision. He sacrificed everything to reach out to that vision — that was very brave, wasn't it? You see what he did was to try to release the soul from his body, even when his body was still alive — '

She turns and the two attendants lay her out upon the trolley and cover her with the sheet.

Music. The Parisian outdoor café scene fully lit.

Four attendants bring on puppets of gentlemen who pass by OSCAR *at his café table.* OSCAR *stretches out his hand to beg. Various reactions from gentlemen puppets as they sweep by. Some give him money, others sweep by contemptuously. Then silence.*

The figure of OSCAR *rises to full height, back to audience, and throws both hands in the air. A piercing sound and light change, high, white spot. At once all the costume, together with the hat and wig, fall off to reveal the naked Androgyne who now poses before the white disk, a flare of white light, then black out and the play ends.*